Thanksgiving Day

Dennis Brindell Fradin

—Best Holiday Books—

ENSLOW PUBLISHERS, INC.

Bloy St. & Ramsey Ave.   P.O. Box 38
Box 777   Aldershot
Hillside, N.J. 07205   Hants GU12 6BP
U.S.A.   U.K.

For my lovely daughter, Diana Judith Fradin

Library of Congress Cataloging-in-Publication Data

Fradin, Dennis B.
    Thanksgiving Day / by Dennis Brindell Fradin.
       p. cm. — (Best holiday books)
Includes index.

    Summary: Describes the historic events that shaped this national day of thanks and details the various ways it is celebrated.

    1. Thanksgiving Day—Juvenile literature. [1. Thanksgiving Day.]
I. Title. II. Series: Fradin, Dennis B. Best holiday books.
GT4975.F73 1990
394.2'683—dc20   89-7680
                                                      CIP
                                                      AC

ISBN 0-89490-236-9

Printed in the United States of America

10 9 8 7 6 5 4 3 2

Illustration Credits:
Cameramann International, Ltd.: pp. 36, 41; Tom Dunnington: p. 28; Courtesy FDR Library: p. 34; Photo by Jerry Hennen: p. 40; Library of Congress: pp. 4, 9, 14, 15, 20, 22, 23, 24, 30, 31; Photographs courtesy of the Rev. Gary L. Marks: pp. 16, 17; Courtesy of The Mount Vernon Ladies' Association: p. 32; National Turkey Federation: p. 44; Photo courtesy of Spertus Museum, Chicago: p. 8.

Cover Illustration by Charlott Nathan

Contents

Home to Thanksgiving, a scene published in 1867 by Currier & Ives

A Very Popular Holiday

A certain Wednesday in November is a very busy travel day in the United States. Airlines have their busiest day of the year. Trains and buses are packed. Highways are crowded.

What is special about this November Wednesday? It is the day before Thanksgiving, which comes on the fourth Thursday in November. Families gather from far and near to spend Thanksgiving Day together. For many families, Thanksgiving is the only time when everyone gathers together.

There are a few Thanksgiving customs. It is a custom to express thanks for your blessings on Thanksgiving Day. The name of the holiday shows that giving thanks is what the day is all about. Many people give thanks at a house of worship or pray with their families at home.

It is also a custom to enjoy a turkey dinner on Thanksgiving. In fact, Thanksgiving is nick-named "Turkey Day."

Thanksgiving has an interesting history. Many people know that the Pilgrims who came to America in 1620 helped start the holiday. But few people know that Thanksgiving's roots go back much farther than the Pilgrims.

Giving Thanks for the Harvest

Long ago, most people grew their own food. They planted seeds in the spring. All summer they tended the plants. If the weather was good, they harvested enough crops in the fall to last all winter.

Farming people around the world held harvest festivals. They did this to thank their gods or God for providing food. Prayer and food were often big parts of these festivals.

The Egyptians held some of the first known thanksgiving festivals over 4,000 years ago. Their festivals honored Min, a nature god. The Egyptians enjoyed food, music, and sports at these celebrations.

The ancient Greek, Roman, Chinese, and Jewish people also had harvest festivals. One of the oldest thanksgiving festivals still being held is called Sukkot. Jewish people began celebrating Sukkot several thousand years ago. Most American Jews who celebrate Sukkot also celebrate Thanksgiving.

Jewish people celebrating Sukkot in the early 1700s. Jews have celebrated this holiday for thousands of years.

In more recent times, people in many lands held thanksgiving festivals. For example, English farmers held the Harvest Home Festival after the grain harvest. They enjoyed feasts, dancing, and games at the Harvest Home Festival.

An old European harvest scene

Giving Thanks for Surviving Hard Times

The harvest season was not the only time that people gathered to give thanks. People have always come together to thank God for guiding them through hard times. Often they proclaimed special days of thanksgiving.

These thanksgivings differed from the harvest festivals. They came at various times of the year. Also, in many cases food was not served. In fact, people often avoided food and spent the whole day praying. Not eating for a time is called fasting.

Thanksgiving in the United States grew out of the Pilgrims' Thanksgiving of 1621. And it in turn was a product of two old traditions. It was partly a fall harvest festival. And it was partly a time when the Pilgrims thanked God for helping them survive.

The Pilgrims Come to America

In the early 1600s, people in England could not worship as they pleased. King James I told all English people to belong to the Church of England. Those who joined other churches could be punished.

Many people left the Church of England anyway. They did so because they felt the Church was ignoring the ideas in the Bible. Those who left the Church of England were called Separatists. They met in barns and homes so that the king would not find out about them.

One Separatist group gathered in Scrooby, England. In 1607 King James's attention turned to Scrooby. Separatists there lost their jobs and were jailed.

In 1608 many of the Scrooby Separatists moved to the Netherlands. The Dutch (people of the Netherlands) welcomed them. But as years passed, the Separatists saw their children losing their English ways. They decided to find a place where they could worship freely while living as English people.

They decided to move to America. Doing so was risky. The ocean voyage was dangerous. Life in the new country would be very hard. By 1620, Virginia was England's only American colony. Most of the English people who had gone to Virginia between 1607 and 1620 had died of hunger or disease. Yet the Separatists were ready to risk death for their faith.

The Separatists returned to England. There some non-Separatists who also wanted to live in America joined them. People who take long religious trips are called pilgrims. The Scrooby Separatists were making a long trip for religious reasons. They and the others who sailed with them became known as the Pilgrims.

The 102 Pilgrims left England on the *Mayflower* on September 16, 1620. They were seasick and cramped on the 3,000-mile voyage. Their food was cold and sometimes rotten. But

The *Mayflower,* which brought the Pilgrims to America

on and on they sailed, going about 50 miles a day.

After 65 days at sea, the Pilgrims reached land. They were in Massachusetts in the New England region. For a month, the Pilgrims looked for a good site for their colony. Finally, they chose to settle at a place called Plymouth.

The landing of the Pilgrims at Plymouth, Massachusetts, in late 1620

Some of the people who became known as the Pilgrims worshiped in this building in Scrooby, England.

It is thought that some of the houses along this street in Leiden, the
Netherlands, were occupied by Pilgrims nearly 400 years ago.

The Indians Befriend the Pilgrims

The Pilgrims chopped down trees. They used the wood to build Plymouth. Few of the Pilgrims knew how to live in the wilderness. About half of them died of hunger and disease during the first winter.

By early spring 1621 Indians had gathered outside the town. The Indians were just curious. But the Pilgrims thought they might be planning to attack. One March day the Pilgrims were talking about protecting the town from the Indians. Suddenly an Indian walked up to them. "Welcome, Englishmen!" he said in English.

His name was Samoset, and he was a chief of Maine's Pemaquid Indians. Samoset had learned English from friendly fishermen. He told the Pilgrims about the Indians in the Massachusetts region. The Pilgrims shared their duck dinner with him. That night Samoset slept in the home of a Pilgrim family.

A few days later, Samoset came to Plymouth with a friend named Squanto. Plymouth was on land where Squanto's people, the Patuxet Indians, had lived. But all the Patuxet Indians except Squanto had died of disease. Squanto was lonely. So he was glad to have the Pilgrims on his homelands.

Squanto arranged for the Pilgrims to meet the region's most powerful Indian. He was Massasoit, chief of the Wampanoags. Massasoit came to Plymouth in March 1621. He and Plymouth Colony governor John Carver made a peace treaty. They vowed that their people would be friends. The Indians and the colonists lived in peace for many years.

Massasoit coming to Plymouth to meet with Governor Carver

The First Thanksgiving

Jamestown, Virginia, had been England's first permanent American town. Plymouth, Massachusetts, was the second. Squanto deserves much of the credit for Plymouth's success. Without him, the Pilgrims might have starved or returned to England.

The Pilgrims' biggest need was food. Squanto taught them how to grow corn. He showed them the best places to fish and hunt. The wheat and other seeds that the Pilgrims had brought from England did poorly. But the corn grew well. The Pilgrims were happy at harvest time. They had corn and fish for the winter, and their hunters were shooting wild turkeys.

The Pilgrims decided to have a thanksgiving. They asked Squanto to join them. Squanto was sent to invite Massasoit and a few other Indians. Meanwhile, the Pilgrim women and girls fixed enough food for about 60 people. Besides the 50 Pilgrims, a few Indians were expected.

Arrival of the first permanent English settlers in America at Jamestown, Virginia, in 1607

But it was the Indians' custom to bring many guests to parties. This showed that they felt close to those giving the party. Massasoit brought about 90 Indians to Plymouth. The Pilgrims had not made enough food! Massasoit solved the problem by sending hunters into the

Sculpture at the U.S. Capitol building that shows Squanto teaching the Pilgrims how to plant corn

The Pilgrims' first Thanksgiving in 1621 as pictured by an artist

woods. They returned with five deer. Now there was enough food for everyone.

This gathering is often called the "first Thanksgiving," with a capital *T*. It was held in the fall of 1621, but we do not know the date. The Pilgrims must have prayed before eating, but details of this are missing. We do not even know the menu. Besides deer meat, there was probably turkey, fish, corn, fruit, puddings, and wine.

The first Thanksgiving lasted several days. When not eating, the Pilgrims and Indians ran races and played games or slept. This gathering inspired our Thanksgiving Day, held each November in the United States. When it ended, though, there were no plans to make Thanksgiving a yearly event.

The Thanksgiving Custom Spreads

The next year, 1622, the harvest was poor. The Pilgrims held no Thanksgiving. The harvest was better in 1623, so the Pilgrims held another Thanksgiving. Massasoit brought dozens of people and a great deal of food. Unfortunately, Squanto had died in 1622.

England built 13 colonies in America. The Thanksgiving custom spread from Massachusetts to other colonies. There was no single date for the holiday. One colony held Thanksgiving in October. Another had it in November. Even within a colony, the date changed from year to year. And the towns in a colony might hold Thanksgiving on different days.

Food and games had been part of the first Thanksgiving. But in most places until the late 1600s, prayer was the main Thanksgiving activity. Some people fasted on the holiday. And several colonies outlawed games on Thanksgiving.

Then in the late 1600s and early 1700s, Thanksgiving in most places became more like the first one. Big dinners and games became customary. In the Pumpkin Race, players pushed pumpkins over a course with wooden spoons. The idea of the Corn Game was to see who could be the first to find and eat hidden ears of corn.

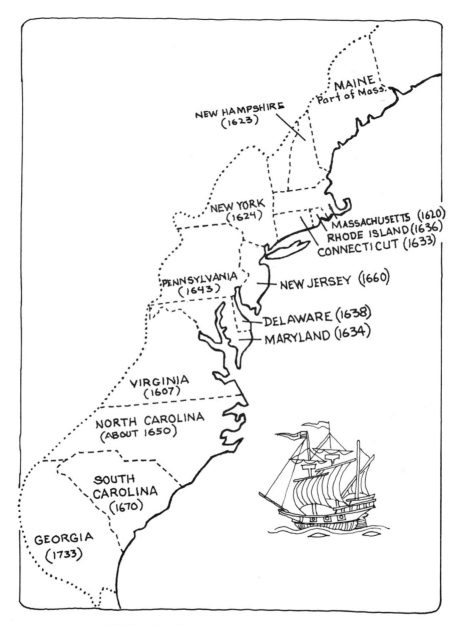

ENGLAND'S 13 AMERICAN COLONIES

The dates show when the colonies were first permanently settled by Europeans.

Thanksgiving Becomes a National Holiday

In 1776 the 13 colonies declared themselves free of England. They called themselves the United States. To win its freedom, the United States had to beat England in the Revolutionary War (1775–1783).

George Washington became the first U.S. president in 1789. President Washington said the whole country should celebrate Thanksgiving on November 26 of that year. The idea of one Thanksgiving Day did not take hold, though. For many years, states still held Thanksgivings on various days.

Sarah Josepha Hale (1788–1879) worked many years to make Thanksgiving a national holiday. Mrs. Hale wrote the poem "Mary Had a Little

Lamb." She also edited a popular magazine. Mrs. Hale ran articles about a national Thanksgiving in her magazine. She wrote letters to lawmakers. Finally, President Abraham Lincoln took her advice.

The year was 1863, and the Civil War was raging. The Northern states fought the Southern states in this war. By fall of 1863, it looked as

Sarah Josepha Hale, who did a great deal to make Thanksgiving a national holiday

though the North would soon win. President Lincoln hoped the North and South would start to make up. He thought a holiday for the whole nation might help. He named the last Thursday in November national Thanksgiving Day.

Many Americans followed Lincoln's order. This marked the start of Thanksgiving as a national U.S. holiday. Each fall for many years

Civil War soldiers pulling on the wishbone to see "who gets their wish." This drawing was made by Winslow Homer in 1864.

after that, the president named a Thanksgiving Day. It was always the last Thursday in November—until 1939.

Portrait of George Washington, the first president

The Fourth Thursday in November

From 1863 to 1938 Thanksgiving had always been the *last* Thursday in November. In 1939 President Franklin D. Roosevelt made a change. He named the *next-to-last* Thursday in November Thanksgiving Day. Many people start their Christmas shopping after Thanksgiving. President Roosevelt wanted people to have more shopping time. That would help businesses.

There was a big uproar. Thanksgiving had been the last Thursday in November for 75 years. Millions of people did not want it to change. Of the 48 states, 23 held Thanksgiving on the day President Roosevelt chose. Another 23 held it on the last Thursday in November.

Texas and Colorado held Thanksgiving on both days!

The U.S. Congress decided that the president should no longer pick Thanksgiving Day. It should be on the same day each year. Congress ruled that Thanksgiving would be on the fourth Thursday in November starting in 1942. It has been held then ever since.

Each year a polio patient ate Thanksgiving dinner with President Franklin Delano Roosevelt and his wife Eleanor. In 1938, Robert Rosenbaum was the lucky person.

Schoolchildren and Thanksgiving

Each year, millions of schoolchildren do Thanksgiving projects. They listen to stories about the Pilgrims. Then they write their own Thanksgiving stories and poems. They sing Thanksgiving songs. Some teachers have their students dress as Pilgrims and Indians and act out the story of the first Thanksgiving.

Many schoolchildren also do Thanksgiving art projects. They may draw pictures of turkeys, Pilgrims, and corn for their class bulletin boards. Turkeys, Pilgrims, and corn are symbols of Thanksgiving. In other words, they remind us of Thanksgiving. Do you know why?

These children are putting up a Thanksgiving bulletin board.

Turkey may have been served at the first Thanksgiving. Wild turkeys were plentiful in colonial times, and turkey was a popular food. The Pilgrim decorations remind us of the people who held the first Thanksgiving. And the corn reminds us that Squanto helped the Pilgrims survive.

Preparing for Thanksgiving at Home

A big dinner is a highlight of Thanksgiving for many families. Turkey is the most popular Thanksgiving food. Other traditional Thanksgiving foods are stuffing, cranberry sauce, sweet potatoes, and pumpkin pie.

Making all that food is a lot of work—especially for a big family. Many families divide up the food preparation. One relative makes the turkey. Others make the cranberry sauce, dessert, and other foods.

Many people decorate their homes for Thanksgiving. Children may bring home their school art projects and put them up. People also decorate their homes with colorful "Indian corn" and plants called gourds.

Turkey Day!

Finally, it is the fourth Thursday in November. Because Thanksgiving is a national holiday, most Americans have the day off. Schools are closed. No mail is delivered. Government offices lock their doors. Nearly all businesses close, or open just part of the day for last-minute shoppers. Schools and some businesses remain closed on Friday. That way people can have a four-day weekend—Thursday, Friday, Saturday, and Sunday.

Thanksgiving is a time for giving thanks and for families to be together. Many families go to a house of worship together before their Thanksgiving dinner. However, fewer people do this today than in years past.

Turkeys are a symbol of Thanksgiving. These are wild turkeys.

A child making a paper turkey as a Thanksgiving decoration. The real turkey tastes better!

Parades are an important part of Thanksgiving for many people. A number of cities hold parades on Thanksgiving or later in the weekend. One interesting parade is held in Plymouth, Massachusetts, where the holiday began. People dressed as Pilgrims walk through the streets. This is known as the "Pilgrims' Progress."

For many people sports and games are a big part of Thanksgiving, just as they were in 1621. Some families enjoy touch football games or other contests. Those who don't play may watch the football game on TV.

In recent years, a very good Thanksgiving custom has grown popular. Many families share their blessings with needy people on Thanksgiving. Some make Thanksgiving meals for poor and sick people. Others ask less fortunate people to join them on Thanksgiving. And some bring treats to police, hospital workers, and others who must work on Thanksgiving.

Around sunset, millions of American families sit down to their Thanksgiving dinners. Many families pray before eating the turkey and other good food. When the turkey is picked clean, there may be one more Thanksgiving activity.

Two children grab the ends of a turkey bone called the "wishbone." Each child makes a wish and pulls until the bone breaks. The one left with the bigger piece will have his or her wish granted—they say. But you aren't supposed to tell anyone your wish, or it won't come true!

Finally, the time comes for Thanksgiving to end. Relatives who live far away must go to the airport or bus station. Children must go to sleep. But isn't it good to know that Thanksgiving will come again next year, on the fourth Thursday in November?

Thanksgiving dinner includes turkey for many American families.

Glossary

blessings—things for which people are grateful

colony—a settlement built by a country beyond its borders

custom—a way of doing things that people teach their children

dozen—twelve

fasting—not eating for a time

harvest—the gathering of crops

million—a thousand thousand (1,000,000)

permanent—lasting

Pilgrims—the people who founded Plymouth, Massachusetts, in 1620

president—an important leader; the United States' main leader is called the president

Separatists—people who left the Church of England

symbols—things that make us think of other things; a turkey is a symbol of Thanksgiving

traditional—the way things were done in the past

treaty—agreement

voyage—this usually means a trip across the sea by ship

wishbone—a Y-shaped bone in a bird's breast

Index